Wild Boar:
Reflections & Resolutions

poems by

Heather Kinney

Finishing Line Press
Georgetown, Kentucky

Wild Boar:
Reflections & Resolutions

Publisher: Leah Maines

Editor: Christen Kincaid

Cover Art: Heather Kinney

Author Photo: Anya Lorenzo

Cover Design: Elizabeth Maines

Printed in the USA on acid-free paper.
Order online: www.finishinglinepress.com
              also available on amazon.com

Author inquiries and mail orders:
Finishing Line Press
P. O. Box 1626
Georgetown, Kentucky 40324
U. S. A.

Table of Contents

For my father,
may your soul rest in peace

Part I: Reflections

Mulberry Tree

I return to the mulberry tree of my youth,
where I spent countless summer days with mulberry stained feet,
fully present within myself and my surroundings,
listening to the birds,
the rustle of leaves, the bending of branches,
the buzz of locust,
watching the work of grasshoppers and ants-
all take place before my eyes.
In these dreams,
sometimes the berries are as big as my palm,
perfectly ripe with bright green leaves.
Other times I am showing friends and strangers how to pick the
best berries.
Each time, a calmness overcomes me,
as if I am getting back to something,
as if I am returning home.
Like when I used to wait for the descent of the sun,
to tell me it was time to go home.
Mom would be calling soon for dinner.
I would hop down from the tree,
my feet sinking into over-ripe berries on the ground.
As I walked toward the back door,
I would turn back and gaze at the mulberry tree,
as if to remind myself what it looked like,
hoping it would stay with me.

Hope Chest

Pictures remind me of the father I lost before his death.
A carpenter, a builder with his hands, but a destroyer with his heart.
My uncle said his problem was he always wanted more.
He always thought he should be farther along and better off.
He never seemed to smile,
at least not in pictures.
He was always hiding something,
more than a missing tooth.
He was hiding from his past.
He was hiding from the pain he put in his arm.
He was hiding from the disappointments he made.

I still have the hope chest he built me when I was five—
the first time he got clean, and I was introduced to the man my father
could be.

The man who taught me how to use a hammer.
The man who would wear a hat when he picked me up from school,
so my friends wouldn't think he was my grandpa.
The man who would later lose all of his belongings,
but manage to keep my picture in his wallet.

Fifteen years later, when he sobered up again,
he built me another from my aunt's grand piano
in his earnest attempt to prove he hadn't given up.

He poured himself into savaging every scrap,
sanding away all the rough edges
that had been neglected for so long.

It was barely recognizable when he was finished:
that worn-out old piano was given a new life.

I keep it in my room, where it collects mostly dust.
Part of me cannot stand the thought of putting anything in it.
My father must have put all his hopes in there when he gave it to me,
for he never could keep from destroying the rest.

Today's Poem[1]

Today is a day I'll never forget.
Today is a day I wish I forgot.
Today is a day of sadness.
Today is a day of real madness.
He is my dad,
and I really must add,
he never calls after all.
Sometimes I cry,
and sometimes the tears are dry,

If he called today,
it would make my day all worthwhile.
So God if you're there, tell him I sincerely love him.
Today is a day I will not stress,
and that is the best of all this mess.

[1] Written at age 11.

How the Other Half Dies

How the other half dies is not the kind of death we're used to.
They put you in a plywood box, handing your belongings to your
loved -ones in a plastic bag,
saying this is what he was worth.
Well, I want the world to know you were worth more than the contents
of your old wallet.
I saw the good in you,
even when you did not see it yourself.
You gave what you could,
even though you often took more than you should.
It's not my place to judge.
You pushed stranger's cars out of snow drifts,
knowing you'd be walking for miles.
You talked to everyone as if they were your friend.
If only they could have done the same for you,
you wouldn't have had to die like that.

Wild Boar[2]

When I heard of your death,
my eyes cried a little, but the clouds did the rest,
showering me with tears I did not have the courage to release.
Walking across town that day reminded me of trying to keep up
with your heavy work boots when I was a kid.
Through mounds of snow and ice, we'd climb
in your silent desperation to show me you'd do anything for me.
And all along I knew, and I tried
and tried to tell you, but you with your noble heart
and spirit as wild as a boar always wanted to do more.
Maybe there was something in your name that made it so you
could never stay.
Your father was the same, and your brothers fought it too.
But you could never be tamed for long,
even when you wanted it,
even though you needed it.
The wind would shake your spirit and you were gone,
only to return when a hard fall brought you back.
Dear father, rest for once.
Rest in peace, for me.

[2]My father's last name, Eberhard, comes from the Germanic word
Everardo, meaning courage and strength of a wild boar.

Good Will: A Philosopher's Dilemma

What makes a man good also makes him bad.
He would do anything for his beloved
beg, steal, lie—does that make him bad?
Or does his undying will make him good?
He would also give you his last dollar.
Does it matter?
He loved you,
even if he couldn't be there,
even if couldn't do all the things he wanted to.
He wanted it, more than anything,
more than anyone.
He tripped on his own infallibility,
his own humanity,
as we all do.
He fell longer and hit harder,
as anyone does who tries to climb too high.

Part II: Resolutions

A Dream

I was on a sandy beach
or maybe it was a desert or a river bank.
Dreams have a way of deceiving me.
It didn't matter where I was; I knew I was alone.
With a big stick in my hand, I drew swirls in the sand
as I danced around, moving in circles, barefoot.
I thought, *this is life. I can do this forever.*
I didn't need anything.
I didn't want anything.
When I awoke, I thought,
if I can be happy there,
I can be happy anywhere.
It's been my resolution ever since.

Morning Hope

Standing in front of the sink on a cold winter morning,
I caught a glimpse of a cardinal on the telephone wire.
It was the first one I saw that year. Its beauty struck me.
Its bright red color contrasted against the white landscape of snow
in the backyard.
Watching him, I smiled. Listening to his song, I relaxed.
Nothing else mattered.
Not the coffee I was about to make, nor the oatmeal,
or the morning paper.
As long as he was there, he had my full attention.
Closing my eyes, I tried to enter his world through his song.
When I opened my eyes, he was gone.
It was then that I noticed the water was still running, so I turned
it off.
Every morning since then, I look for him in the backyard,
my morning hope.

Faith

I pray for the insistence of the squirrel,
believing in the future,
working frantically, but diligently to store food for winter,
not caring that he will not reap all of its rewards.
He gives his all each day, and does not ask for more.

Sacred Rituals

Fog rolls in over the foothills of the Appalachian Mountains,
leaves flutter and fall, scattering themselves on the forest floor
birds sing, paying tribute to the rising sun.
The day seems to have just begun, but
it never really ended.
My eyes may have been closed, but
nature keeps moving, keep working
in ways that I will never fully know, but
am learning to appreciate,
and pay tribute to myself.

A Resolution

We shape history every day,
when we move forward towards the rising sun.
Let the day be our guide
may we listen to its melody,
feel its rhythm, singing in tune;
may we find a place in the orchestra
of the natural world;
may we greet each day with good intentions,
kind deeds, and gratefulness,
striving each day to show more compassion
to our fellows,
giving more of ourselves than we formerly thought possible;
may we be open to learn,
willing to make mistakes, eager to help, and humble enough to
apologize;
may we recognize the beauty in every day and night,
and want nothing more.

Rising Storm

The earthworms emerge,
spiders nest, fish feast before retreat.
The brewers flock from limb to limb.

The clouds roll in.

The bees are at their hive.
A cool breeze whistles through the trees as leaves
bend and fold with the wind.

Wolves howl at the sky as the air thickens.
Below ants scurry to protect their mound.
Rain hits my face and I abide.

Grasshopper

I sit and gaze at the fire,
watching a grasshopper who must have been as mesmerized by fire as I
am,
leaping over it back and forth,
dancing dazzlingly with the flame.

I move closer.

Another grasshopper, maybe its young, just watches,
with its antenna inching closer and closer and then away and back again,
wanting to dance with the flame, like its mother, but cautious all the
same.

The dancing one in the most beautiful step, slipped into the flame,
twirling about the light, spinning and swirling in cadence with the wind-
until her number ended,
and she laid on her back;
her legs still twitching.

I move closer.

The little one was still watching.

Oh, to be young and so patient, and oh
  to be older and so daring.

I move closer,
wanting to tell the little one to stay away from the flame.

I watch the little one move its antenna forward and then back again.

I move closer and with one swift blow,
I put the fire out.

Red Maples

Across the hollow, red maples are the first to turn in fall.
Their crimson peaks from the highest treetops,
reminding me that all leaves will soon turn and fall.
And how beautiful process is.
Autumn is a time of change, of shedding what no longer suits us.
The red maple stands alone for a while,
but the others will change too- yellow and orange maples, and
All shades in between,
calling to our attention:
all that once looked like a sea of green in the distance
will make its name known before it rests for winter.

Wild Boar, part II

Perhaps I was too young, before now
to understand how death reveals hidden truths.
Not only the dark secrets swept under the rug,
but also the light that we never bothered to look for.
All the questions we failed to ask those we love
      linger somewhere in our bodies.

I felt that longing before my father was actually gone.
Maybe I always felt that longing with him.
Because I felt like I never really had him.
He was too far away, even when he was sitting
across from me at the local deli.

We understand ourselves better through the history of our blood and
bones.
      About how grandpa hunted deer and pheasant, but mostly squirrel.
      About how dad quietly went to Mass, alone.

I have come to understand myself differently, now
after my father's death.
I always thought of myself as my mother's daughter.
After all, I went by her last name,
a symbol I have worn with pride.
But death calls you to question parts of yourself you
didn't want to look at before.

Like the fact that I am my father's daughter, too.
Not only in blood and memory, but in public record.
The name Eberhard—his name is on my birth certificate.
I am the daughter of a wild one, a wild boar,
and that spirit of restlessness resides in my bones.

I understand perhaps a little bit more
of my father's wayfaring ways.
I just hope it's enough to keep me from drifting too far,
from destroying too much of what I love.

Winter

On a cold crisp morning, so bare and lonely,
an emptiness presides in the air.
that stillness that only February knows.
what dwells beneath the snow is a mystery;
what slumbers beneath the frozen soil will not be known for months.
Rest and wait-
In the meantime,
farmers and gardeners, the believers in the future,
the gamblers of an uncertain fate, the patient ones,
prepare for another season, another spring to emerge,
that opening in the earth and of the soul and mind,
that fills the air with a breath of new life.
winter, that brutish once unforgiving friend, makes it possible.

Heather Kinney is a writer. She resides in Lexington, Kentucky. This is her first published work.